أيّها الـ سمر، أُسمر،
ماذا ترى؟

Brown Bear, Brown Bear,
What Do You See?

Pictures by Eric Carle

أيّها الدّب الأسمر، أيّها الدّب الأسمر،
ماذا ترى؟

Brown Bear, Brown Bear,
What Do You See?

by Bill Martin, Jr.
Arabic translation by Dr. Sajida Fawzi

Mantra Lingua

أيّها الدّب الأسمر، أيّها الدّب الأسمر،
ماذا ترى؟

Brown bear, brown bear,
what do you see?

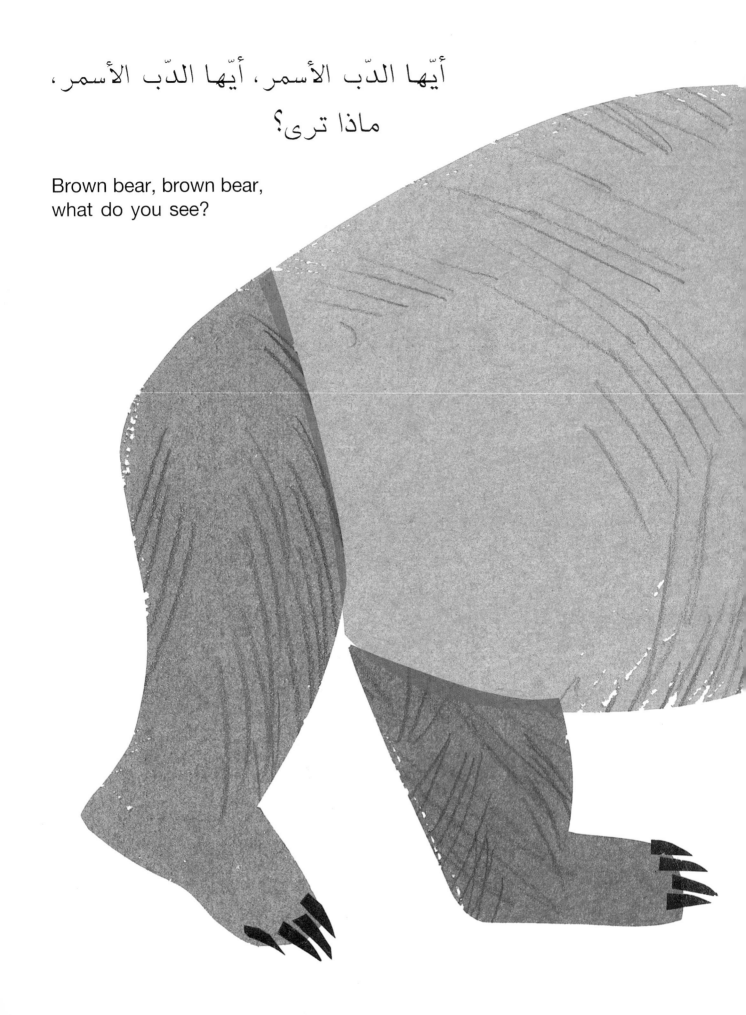

أرى طيراً أحمر
ينظر إليّ.

I see a red bird
looking at me.

أيّها الطير الأحمر،
أيها الطير الأحمر،
ماذا ترى؟

Red bird, red bird,
what do you see?

أرى بطّة صفراء
ينظر إليّ.

I see a yellow duck
looking at me.

أيّها البطة الصفراء،
أيّها البطة الصفراء، ماذا ترين؟

Yellow duck, yellow duck, what do you see?

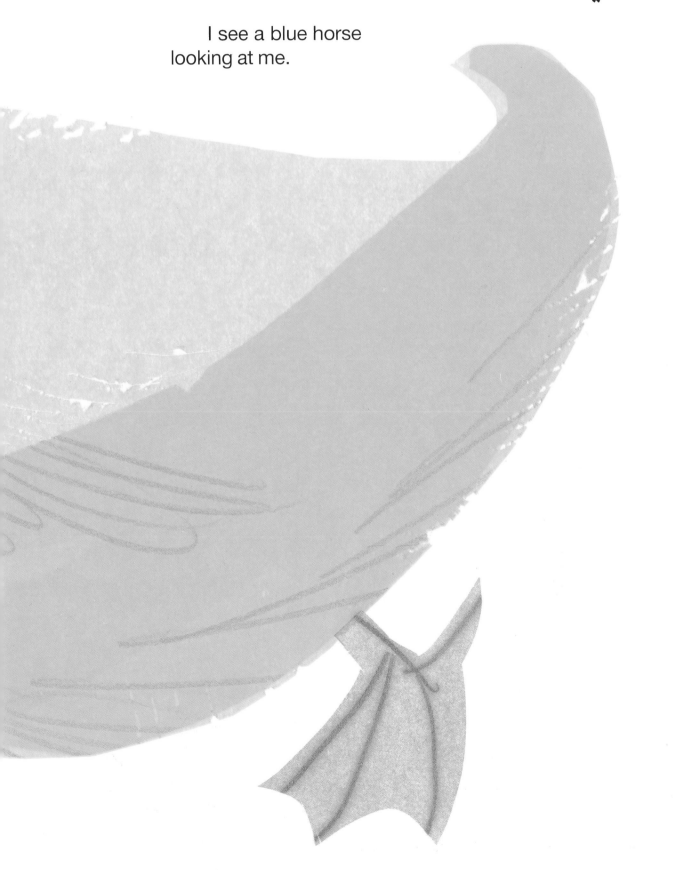

أرى حصانا أزرق
ينظر إليّ.

I see a blue horse
looking at me.

أيّها الحصان الأزرق،
أيّها الحصان الأزرق،
ماذا ترى؟

Blue horse, blue horse,
what do you see?

أرى ضفدعة خضراء
تنظر إليّ.

I see a green frog
looking at me.

أيّها الضفدعة الخضراء،
أيّها الضفدعة الخضراء، ماذا ترين؟

Green frog, green frog,
what do you see?

أرى قطة بنفسجيّة
تنظر إليّ.

I see a purple cat
looking at me.

أيّها القطة البنفسجيّة،
أيّها القطة البنفسجيّة، ماذا ترين؟

Purple cat, purple cat,
what do you see?

أرى كلباً أبيض
ينظر إليّ.

I see a white dog
looking at me.

أيّها الكلب الأبيض، أيّها الكلب الأبيض، ماذا ترى؟

White dog, white dog, what do you see?

أرى خروفاً أسود ينظر إليّ.

I see a black sheep looking at me.

أيّها الخروف الأسود، أيها الخروف الأسود، ماذا ترى؟

Black sheep, black sheep,
what do you see?

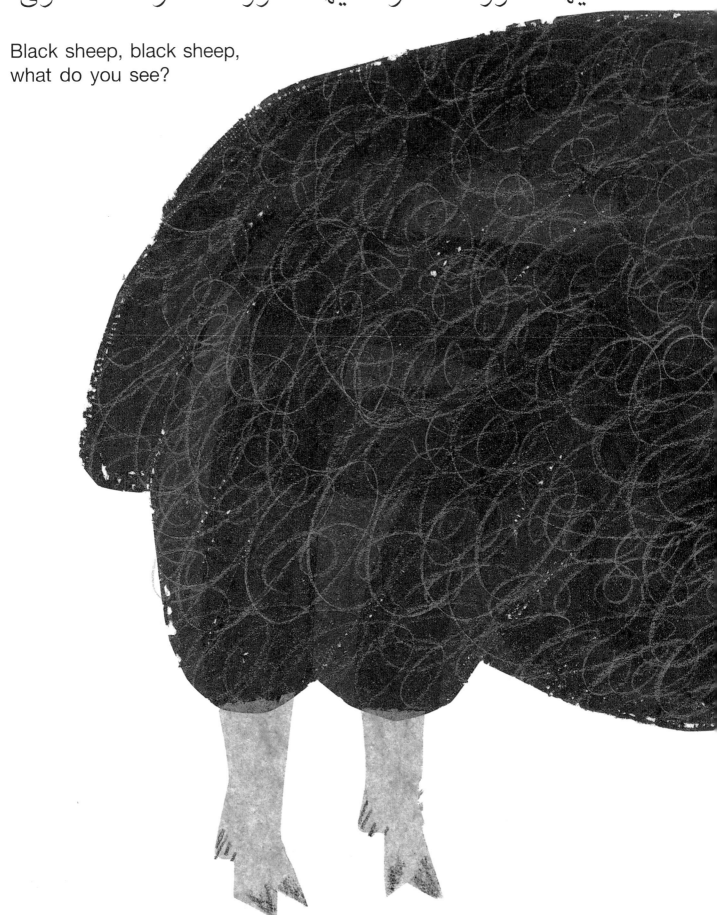

أرى سمكة ذهبيّة
تنظر إليّ.

I see a goldfish
looking at me.

أيّها السمكة الذهبيّة،
أيّها السمكة الذهبيّة، ماذا ترين؟

Goldfish, goldfish,
what do you see?

أرى قرداً
ينظر إليّ.

I see a monkey
looking at me.

أيّها القرد، أيّها القرد،
ماذا ترى؟

Monkey, monkey,
what do you see?

أيّها القرد، أيّها القرد،

أرى أطفالاً
ينظرون إليّ.

I see children
looking at me.

أيّها الأطفال، أيّها الأطفال،
ماذا ترون؟

Children, children,
what do you see?

We see a brown bear   نرى دُبّاً أسمر

a red bird   طيراً أحمر

a green frog   ضفدعة خضراء

a black sheep   خروفاً أسود

a goldfish   سمكة ذهبيّة

a yellow duck   بطّة صفراء

a blue horse   حصاناً أزرق

a purple cat   قطّة بنفسجيّة

a white dog   كلباً أبيض

وقرداً ينظر إلينا.

هذا ما نراه.

and a monkey looking at us.
That's what we see.

Text copyright © 1967, 1983 Holt Rinehart and Winston
Illustration copyright © 1984 Eric Carle
Dual language copyright © 2004 Mantra Lingua

This edition 2015

ISBN 978 1 84444 116 7

A CIP record for this book is available from the British Library

First published in dual language in Great Britain 2004 by Mantra Lingua Ltd
Global House, 303 Ballards Lane, London N12 8NP, UK
www.mantralingua.com

Printed in Paola,Malta MP210815PB09151167